The Business 2.0

B1 PRE-INTERMEDIATE

e Workbook

Contents

The **Business** 2.0

The Business 2.0 eWorkbook combines the best of both worlds: everything you would find in a printed Workbook and multimedia resources to enhance revision and ongoing learning.

The Business 2.0 eWorkbooks are mainly intended for self-study or home study. They contain a set of resources to support and enhance the material in the Student's Book. The eWorkbook can be used with your computer or you can save some of the material and use it with other devices (for example, mp3 players and smartphones).

If you prefer to work on paper you can also print your work.

When you launch a level of *The Business 2.0* eWorkbook you will see the following options:

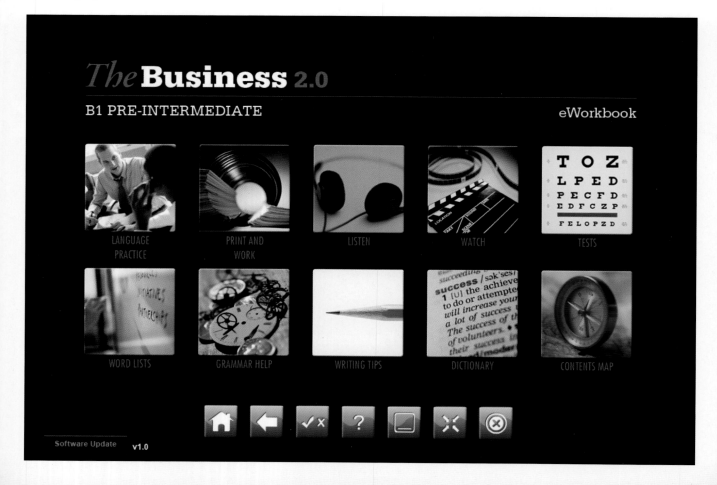

Contents map

Where to start?

You can start by going to help 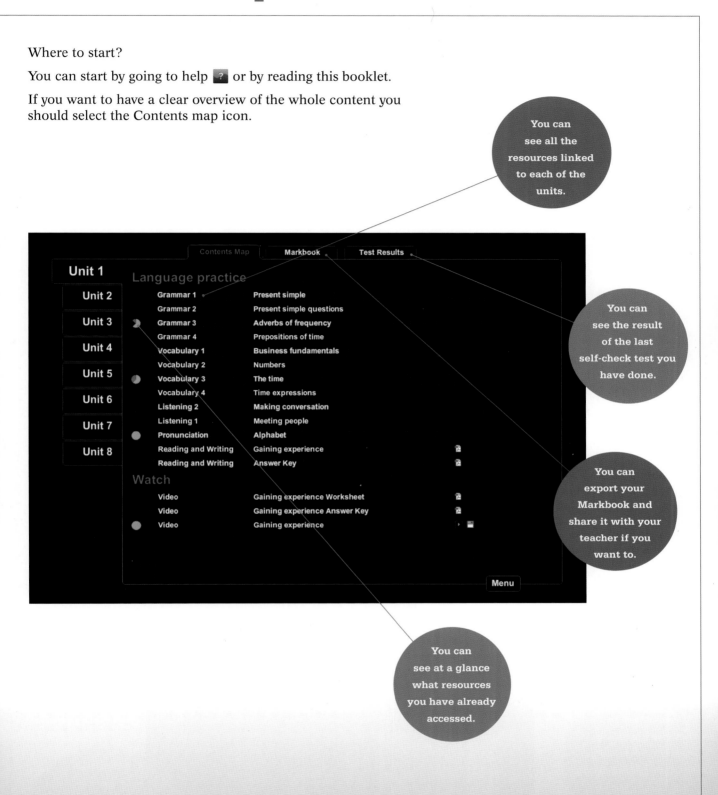 or by reading this booklet.

If you want to have a clear overview of the whole content you should select the Contents map icon.

You can see all the resources linked to each of the units.

Contents Map   **Markbook**   **Test Results**

Unit 1

Language practice

Unit 2	Grammar 1	Present simple
Unit 3	Grammar 2	Present simple questions
	Grammar 3	Adverbs of frequency
Unit 4	Grammar 4	Prepositions of time
	Vocabulary 1	Business fundamentals
Unit 5	Vocabulary 2	Numbers
	Vocabulary 3	The time
Unit 6	Vocabulary 4	Time expressions
	Listening 2	Making conversation
Unit 7	Listening 1	Meeting people
	Pronunciation	Alphabet
Unit 8	Reading and Writing	Gaining experience
	Reading and Writing	Answer Key

Watch

Video	Gaining experience Worksheet
Video	Gaining experience Answer Key
Video	Gaining experience

Menu

You can see the result of the last self-check test you have done.

You can export your Markbook and share it with your teacher if you want to.

You can see at a glance what resources you have already accessed.

Language practice

LANGUAGE PRACTICE

The Language practice section includes activities that provide consolidation of the language presented in the Student's Book. It includes all the language skills: grammar, vocabulary, listening, pronunciation, reading and writing.

One of the advantages of the eWorkbook is that you can do the exercises as many times as you want. Most of the exercises are interactive. Reading and Writing activities are printable PDFs.

If you choose to work by skill, you will be taken to a list of all the different activities related to that particular skill.

If you choose to work by unit, you will be taken to a list of all the activities related to that particular unit.

When you choose an activity practising grammar, vocabulary, listening or pronunciation you will be taken to a screen like this one.

Whichever way you work you will always be able to access the following resources: Dictionary, Grammar Help, Word Lists and Writing Tips.

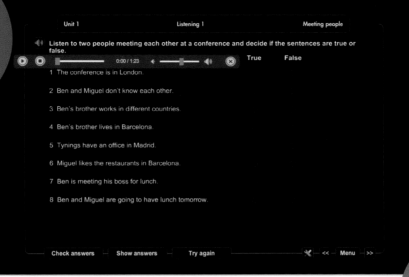

The Business 2.0

Unit 1 Reading and writing: Gaining experience

Reading

Informal emails

1 Read the informal email below and answer these questions.

1 Who wrote the email?
2 Who is the recipient?
3 What is the subject of the email?
4 Is this the first email Pete has sent to Suzy?
5 What date and time will Pete arrive?
6 What three requests does Pete make to Suzy?
7 What is Pete doing this weekend?
8 Can Pete check his emails during this time?
9 Have Pete and Suzy met each other?

✉	INBOX	REPLY ←	FORWARD →

From:	Pete Simpson
Sent:	4 June 2013
To:	Suzy Marks
Subject:	Arrival in Japan

The Business 2.0

Unit 8 Reading and writing: Global trade

2 Complete the sentences with the best words in **bold** from the progress report.

1 Our recent results are very exciting, as turnover increased last year. _____ there were lower costs.
2 _____ this is an urgent issue, I have already contacted the area managers.
3 Four out of six visits were cancelled. _____, we only met two suppliers.
4 _____ our main supplier went bankrupt, we were able to source sufficient stock.
5 _____ we need to recruit staff as soon as possible, we will start interviewing immediately.
6 Some franchisees cannot get a business loan. We should _____ provide a loan arrangement.
7 We plan to complete the project early. _____, the project is under budget.
8 _____ the lawyer was very expensive, we were very pleased with his work.

Writing

Write a progress report

3 You work for a company that wants to open six new franchises in China. You are looking for suitable franchisees. Write a progress report. Include the following information.

- background of the project
- current situation
- problems experienced
- action plan and conclusion.

Print and work

PRINT AND WORK

This section offers a pen-and-paper version of the activities in the Language practice section, plus downloadable audio tracks when needed. It is designed to suit a different learning style. If you prefer to work away from the computer, this gives you exactly what you would expect in a printed workbook with the added advantage that you only print the pages that you need.

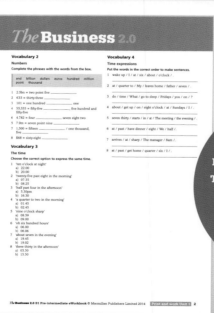

The content is the same as in the Language practice section. The only small changes are related to how you do the activity. For example, it may say 'underline' instead of 'click'.

The Business 2.0

B1 PRE-INTERMEDIATE

eWorkbook

PRINT AND WORK

Unit 1   Gaining experience

Grammar, Vocabulary, Listening, Pronunciation

Answer key

Audioscript

If audio files are needed to complete an activity, you can easily access these and listen to them.

There is an answer key provided as a PDF.

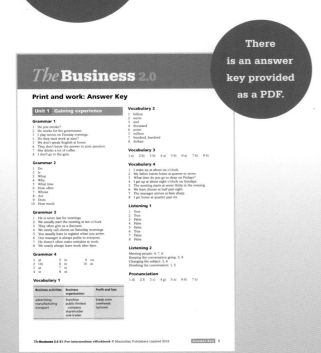

The Business 2.0

Print and work: Answer Key

Unit 1   Gaining experience

Grammar 1
1 Do you smoke?
2 He works for the government.
3 I play tennis on Tuesday evenings.
4 Do they start work at nine?
5 We don't speak English at home.
6 They don't know the answer to your question.
7 She drinks a lot of coffee.
8 I don't go to the gym.

Grammar 2
1 Do
2 Is
3 What
4 Why
5 What time
6 How often
7 Whose
8 Are
9 Does
10 How much

Grammar 3
1 He is never late for meetings.
2 We usually start the meeting at ten o'clock.
3 They often give us a discount.
4 We rarely call clients on Saturday mornings.
5 You usually have to register when you arrive.
6 Our manager is always polite to everyone.
7 He doesn't often make mistakes at work.
8 We nearly always leave work after 8pm.

Grammar 4
1 at   5 in   9 on
2 On   6 in   10 at
3 at   7 in
4 in   8 at

Vocabulary 1

Business activities	Business organization	Profit and loss
advertising manufacturing transport	franchise public limited company shareholder sole trader	break even overheads turnover

Vocabulary 2
1 billion
2 euros
3 and
4 thousand
5 point
6 million
7 hundred, hundred
8 dollars

Vocabulary 3
1 a)   2 b)   3 b)   4 a)   5 b)   6 a)   7 b)   8 b)

Vocabulary 4
1 I wake up at about six o'clock.
2 My father leaves home at quarter to seven.
3 What time do you go to sleep on Fridays?
4 I get up at about eight o'clock on Sundays.
5 The meeting starts at seven thirty in the evening.
6 We have dinner at half past eight.
7 The manager arrives at 8am sharp.
8 I get home at quarter past six.

Listening 1
1 True
2 True
3 False
4 False
5 True
6 True
7 False
8 False

Listening 2
Meeting people: 4, 7, 8
Keeping the conversation going: 3, 9
Changing the subject: 2, 6
Finishing the conversation: 1, 5

Pronunciation
1 d)   2 f)   3 c)   4 g)   5 a)   6 b)   7 e)

There is an audioscript provided as a PDF.

The Business 2.0

Print and work: Audioscript

Unit 1

Listening 1 & 2
B: Excuse me, is this seat free?
M: Yes, it is.
B: Great, thanks. My name's Ben. I'm with Tynings here in London. Our office is just round the corner. Nice to meet you.
M: Nice to meet you, too. I'm Miguel. I'm from Armada in Spain.
B: Spain? Really?
M: Yes.
B: It's a beautiful country. My brother lives there with his wife. He's freelance and works for different companies.
M: Uh-huh?
B: They live in Madrid. They both speak Spanish very well. Enough about them, let's talk about you. Where are you from?
M: Barcelona.
B: I see. That's a great city. Tynings have an office there. I love the restaurants there, don't you?
M: Yes. The restaurants are very good. Anyway, I have a meeting with my boss now.
B: Listen, talking of restaurants, do you have time for lunch? There's a lovely tapas restaurant near here. I'm meeting my colleagues there.
M: Sorry, maybe tomorrow. Do excuse me, I really must go.
B: OK. It was nice meeting you, Miguel.
M: Good to meet you, too.

Pronunciation
1 /ɒ/
2 /ɪ/
3 /e/
4 /æ/
5 /əʊ/
6 /ɑː/
7 /ɑː/

Unit 2

Listening 1 & 2
R: City Spa. Good morning. Can I help you?
A: Good morning. Could I speak to Sally Anderson, please?
R: Could I have your name, please?
A: This is Alex Smithers from Waterford Brothers.
R: Just a moment please, Mr Smithers.
R: I'm sorry, Mr Smithers. She isn't answering. Would you like to speak to her assistant, Tina?
A: Yes, please.
R: I'll put you through now.
A: Thank you.
T: Tina Balding.
A: Hello Tina. It's Alex, from Waterford Brothers. How are you?
T: Good, thanks. And you, Alex?
A: I'm fine, thanks. Is Sally there?
T: I'm sorry. She isn't working this morning. Can I take a message?
A: Yes, please. I'm calling about the customer service training Sally wanted to book. Do you know which dates she wants?
T: I'm not sure. Would you like me to get her to call you back?
A: Yes, please.
T: I'll ask her to get back to you as soon as she arrives.
A: Great. Thanks for your help, Tina.
T: You're welcome.
A: Goodbye.
T: Bye.

Pronunciation
1 Could I exchange this software? (✓)
2 I'm sorry, but the computer systems aren't working. (✓)
3 Can you call me back later, please? (✗)
4 I'm sorry, She isn't working early this afternoon. (✗)
5 Can you help me with this query, please? (✓)
6 I'm sorry, but I'm preparing these important documents. (✗)
7 Could I speak to the manager? (✗)
8 I'm sorry, but she's giving a presentation at the moment. (✓)

Listen

This section offers access to all the listening material in the eWorkbook. It includes the following:

- Access to the listening and pronunciation activities in the Language Practice section.

- Audio material designed to be used 'on the move', including all the Student's Book class audio.

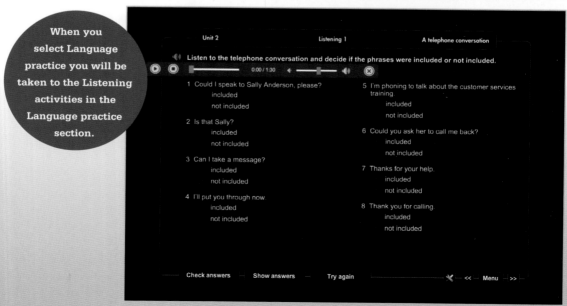

When you select Language practice you will be taken to the Listening activities in the Language practice section.

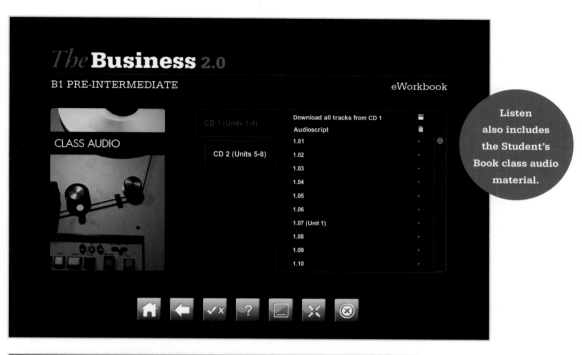

Listen also includes the Student's Book class audio material.

You can play this material by clicking on play or you can download the files and copy them onto an mp3 player or other devices.

You can also print or download a PDF with the audioscript for all this material.

Watch

WATCH

When you select Watch in the main menu you are taken to a screen where all the video clips in the eWorkbook are listed. You can either watch the videos on your computer or download the files.

When you click on 'download' you can copy the files to a selected location. You can download the files in a number of formats, for example for smartphones, tablets, mp3 players or other common mobile devices.

There are accompanying worksheets, available as printable PDFs, one per unit. These include comprehension questions, language work and follow-up tasks. These can be used when you watch the video material on your computer or on the move.

There is an answer key and video script provided as a PDF for each video worksheet. These are also downloadable.

There is one video clip per unit. The video clips illustrate the communication and people skills featured in each unit.

Reference tools

The Business 2.0 eWorkbook contains powerful Reference tools to help you with your work.

These tools can be accessed directly from the main menu on the home page or when you are doing an activity.

DICTIONARY   WORD LISTS   GRAMMAR HELP   WRITING TIPS

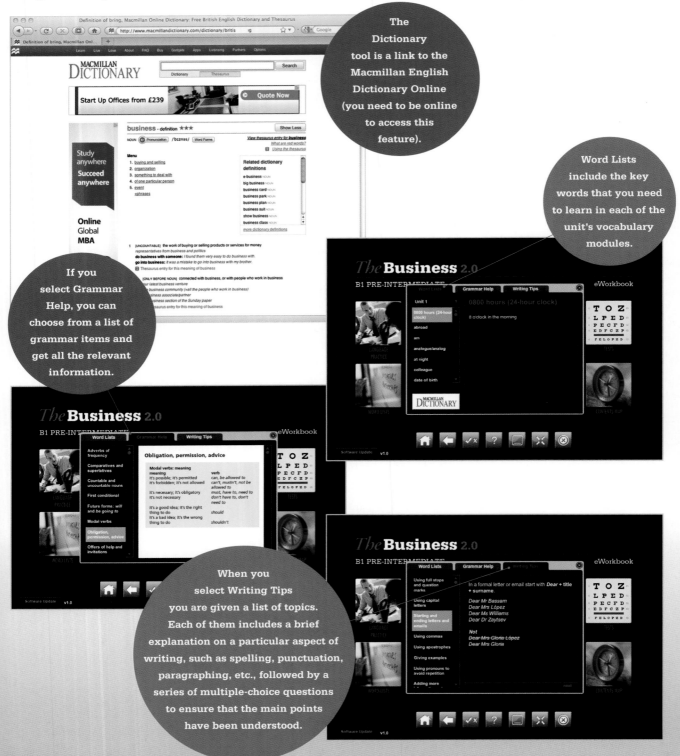

The Dictionary tool is a link to the Macmillan English Dictionary Online (you need to be online to access this feature).

Word Lists include the key words that you need to learn in each of the unit's vocabulary modules.

If you select Grammar Help, you can choose from a list of grammar items and get all the relevant information.

When you select Writing Tips you are given a list of topics. Each of them includes a brief explanation on a particular aspect of writing, such as spelling, punctuation, paragraphing, etc., followed by a series of multiple-choice questions to ensure that the main points have been understood.

Tests

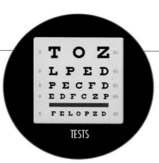

TESTS

You can test yourself at any point using *The Business 2.0* eWorkbook. You can set yourself tests either by a set time or a set number of questions.

When you finish the test you will be given a score. Your last three scores will be recorded.

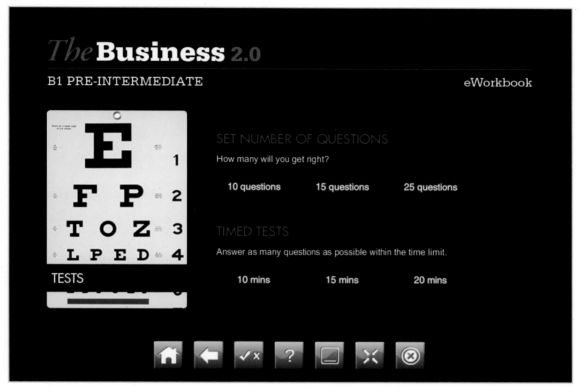

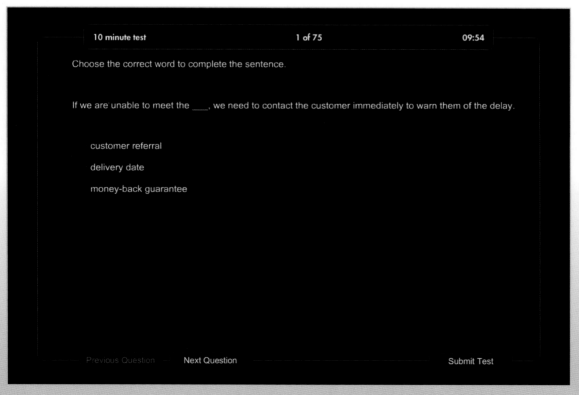

Installation instructions

To install and run *The Business 2.0 eWorkbook*

Windows

Insert the DVD-ROM and choose 'Run' from the auto play menu.

Macintosh

Please select the DVD-ROM drive and double click Install from the Install_Mac folder. Follow the on-screen instructions.

Once installed, you may wish to drag the application icon from the applications folder to your dock for easy access.

Alternatively, double click the application from the applications folder to launch.

Trouble installing your eWorkbook?

Go to the *Macmillan Product Support* website at http://help.macmillan.com

You'll find a section that deals with problems that a small number of users have reported.

Recommended System Requirements

Windows

Processor: Pentium 4, 3ghz or Intel Core 2 Duo

Hard disk: Minimum 2 GB free, 3 GB free on the system drive

Operating systems: Vista, XP SP2, Windows 7

32 MB Video RAM

2 GB RAM

Audio sound card

DVD drive

Internet Connection (For Registration/live updates)

System administration rights for installation

Macintosh

Intel Core™ Duo 1.33 GHz or faster processor

2 GB RAM

32 MB video RAM

Operating systems: Mac OS X v.10.4 or later

Hard disk: Minimum 2 GB free, 3 GB free on the system Drive

DVD Drive Internet connection (For Registration/live updates)

System administration rights for installation

Minimum System Requirements

Windows

Processor: Pentium 4, 2ghz or faster

Hard disk: Minimum 2 GB free, 3 GB free on the system drive

Operating systems: Vista, XP SP2, Windows 7

32 MB Video RAM

1 GB RAM Audio sound card

DVD drive

Internet Connection (For Registration/live updates)

System administration rights for installation

Macintosh

Intel Core™ Duo 1.33 GHz or faster processor

1 GB RAM

32 MB video RAM

Operating systems: Mac OS X v.10.4 or later

Hard disk: Minimum 2 GB free, 3 GB free on the system drive

DVD drive

Internet connection (For registration/live updates)

System administration rights for installation

Important Information

Appropriate rights are required to install software on your computer and to write end-user data to your computer's hard disk. If end-user rights are restricted, it might not be possible to save the results score in the activities. Please seek expert advice if you do not have the necessary rights.

If you have obtained your Macmillan DVD-ROM from an authorised supplier, then our software is guaranteed to contain no viruses or similar threats. If you have any doubts about the authenticity of your DVD-ROM, please consult your supplier.

A security program can occasionally report a false alarm, also known as a false positive. When this occurs, the program mistakenly thinks there is a threat, although no threat exists.

If a false alarm is reported, please send details to help@macmillan.com and include the name and version of your security program. A screenshot or image of the problem is helpful too. Please also send the title, ISBN, and version number that are printed on the label of your DVD-ROM, and the name and version of your operating system. We will then attempt to have the virus definition database that is used by the security program updated as quickly as possible.

All Macmillan DVD-ROMs are copyright. Copying is prohibited. Any attempt to copy this DVD-ROM will violate the licence agreement, invalidate the warranty, and cancel your entitlement to customer service and technical support.

END USER SOFTWARE LICENCE AGREEMENT

(SLA) between the company which is granting this licence ("Macmillan Publishers Limited") and end-user ("Licensee"). By installing this Software product you agree to this licence.

1. DEFINITIONS

"**Software**" means the computer programs provided to Licensee by Macmillan and/or computer programs in which Macmillan has proprietary rights and/or sublicence rights granted by a third party licensor, and any related materials or documents, and any subsequent revisions provided to Licensee. "**Configuration**" means central processing unit ("CPU") or any group of CPUs, connected by a local area network, that operate together for the purpose of performing the functions of the Software and/or restricting the use of the Software to the maximum number of licensed users.

2. SCOPE OF AUTHORISED USE

2.1 You may install this software in up to two computers. The Software is furnished under a personal, non-transferable, non-exclusive licence in executable/object code solely for Licensee's own use. Further installations than those defined above may become chargeable. Please contact Macmillan if you require additional licensed copies of this application
2.2 Licensee shall not copy nor permit any party to copy Software, except to make a single copy solely for backup or archival purposes as necessary for use on the Configuration, but only with the inclusion of copyright and proprietary notices. If Licensee is unable to operate Software on the Configuration due to an equipment malfunction, the Software may be used temporarily on another Configuration during the period of equipment malfunction. Licensee shall not sublicense or transfer or otherwise make Software available to any third party. Licensee shall not modify, decompile, disassemble or otherwise reverse engineer Software or create derivative works based on the Software. The Licensee may only exercise rights under s50 of the Copyright Designs and Patents Act 1988 or similar legislation if it has first asked Macmillan to disclose the required information and Macmillan has declined to do so.
2.3 Licensee shall allow Macmillan and its nominated representatives reasonable access to its premises to audit Licensee's compliance with this Agreement.

3. TITLE AND OWNERSHIP; CONFIDENTIALITY

Title to, ownership of the Software and any patent, copyright, underlying trade secret and other intellectual property rights in it or any of its parts shall not transfer to Licensee but shall remain in Macmillan or its third party licensors. Software is confidential and proprietary to Macmillan and/or its third party licensors and Licensee shall observe the proprietary nature thereof. Licensee shall not disclose, provide or otherwise make available Software or any part (which includes without limitation, database structures and message formats) or copies thereof to any third party. Licensee shall take action by instruction or agreement with its employees who are permitted access to Software, to protect the confidentiality of Software. Licensee shall keep Software and such materials secure, and prevent unauthorised access, copying or use thereof. Licensee agrees to notify Macmillan immediately it becomes aware of any unauthorised knowledge, possession, or use of Software or any such materials by any person or entity. Additional terms may apply where the Software is owned by a third party and provided by Macmillan under licence; in such cases, those terms will be provided separately.

4. LIMITED WARRANTY

A. Macmillan warrants that all unmodified Software, when used under the conditions described in the applicable Macmillan published specifications furnished to Licensee, if any, will conform to said Macmillan published specifications at time of shipment and for a period of ninety (90) days. If Licensee determines that a non-conformity exists which is a substantial deviation from the Macmillan published specification, Licensee shall provide proper written notification to Macmillan, within the warranty period, explaining the alleged nonconformity. Upon receipt of such written notification Macmillan's or its third party Licensors' sole liability and Licensee's sole and exclusive remedy shall be for Macmillan to use reasonable efforts to provide, at no cost to Licensee, programming corrections by telephone and/or mail to correct such documented nonconformity. Provided Macmillan determines that the alleged nonconformity is a defect in the unaltered version of the Software and is not the result of (i) Licensee's use of the Software other than in accordance with the Macmillan published specification; or (ii) modifications to the Software made by parties other than Macmillan; or (iii) damage due to improper use or neglect, Macmillan shall use reasonable efforts to remedy such nonconformity by issuing corrected information to Licensee, including corrected documentation or code or a work-around if available. Macmillan does not warrant that the operation of Software will be uninterrupted or error free or that all errors will be remedied. Macmillan does not warrant that Software will meet Licensee's specific requirements or operate with any hardware or software other than as specified in the Macmillan published specification, if any shall have been provided.
B. Macmillan does not warrant the performance of Macmillan products if used with third party products not approved by Macmillan.
C. NEITHER MACMILLAN NOR ANY OF ITS THIRD PARTY LICENSORS MAKES ANY OTHER REPRESENTATION OR WARRANTY REGARDING THE SOFTWARE, INCLUDING EXPRESS OR IMPLIED WARRANTIES OF SATISFACTORY QUALITY, MERCHANTABILITY AND FITNESS FOR A PARTICULAR PURPOSE AND NONINFRINGEMENT OF THIRD PARTY RIGHTS AND ALL OTHER WARRANTIES ARE HEREBY EXPRESSLY DISCLAIMED. SOME JURISDICTIONS DO NOT ALLOW THE EXCLUSION OF IMPLIED WARRANTIES, SO THE ABOVE LIMITATIONS MAY NOT APPLY TO YOU. LICENSEE RETAINS FULL CONTROL OVER AND RESPONSIBILITY FOR THE USE OF SOFTWARE. MACMILLAN DOES NOT WARRANT THE MERCHANTABILITY OF ANY OF LICENSEE'S PRODUCTS THROUGH THE USE OF THE SOFTWARE. THIS WARRANTY GIVES YOU SPECIFIC LEGAL RIGHTS. YOU MAY HAVE OTHER RIGHTS, WHICH VARY FROM JURISDICTION TO JURISDICTION.

5. LIMITATION OF LIABILITY

IN NO EVENT IS MACMILLAN OR ITS THIRD PARTY LICENSORS LIABLE FOR DAMAGES INCLUDING, BUT NOT LIMITED TO LOSS OF PROFITS, OPPORTUNITY, DATA OR FOR INDIRECT, INCIDENTAL, SPECIAL OR CONSEQUENTIAL DAMAGES ARISING OUT OF OR IN CONNECTION WITH THE USE OR PERFORMANCE OF SOFTWARE, EVEN IF NOTICE HAS BEEN GIVEN OF THE POSSIBILITY OF SUCH DAMAGES. THIS LIMITATION OF LIABILITY SHALL NOT APPLY TO LIABILITY FOR FRAUD AND DEATH OR PERSONAL INJURY RESULTING FROM MACMILLAN'S NEGLIGENCE TO THE EXTENT APPLICABLE LAW PROHIBITS SUCH LIMITATION. SOME JURISDICTIONS DO NOT ALLOW EXCLUSIONS OR LIMITATIONS LIABILITY, SO THIS EXCLUSION AND LIMITATION MAY NOT APPLY TO YOU. IN NO EVENT WILL MACMILLAN OR ITS THIRD PARTY LICENSORS BE LIABLE FOR ANY AMOUNT GREATER THAN THE INITIAL LICENCE FEE PAID FOR THE SOFTWARE WHICH ALLEGEDLY CAUSED THE DAMAGE, EVEN IF MACMILLAN SHALL HAVE BEEN INFORMED OF SUCH DAMAGES OR OF ANY CLAIM BY ANY THIRD PARTY.

6. INFRINGEMENT INDEMNITY

Macmillan shall defend any action, suit or proceeding brought against Licensee which alleges that any Macmillan proprietary Software infringes a U.S. or U.K. patent or copyright that Macmillan is aware of, on the condition that Licensee promptly notifies Macmillan of the action and gives Macmillan the opportunity, full authority, information and assistance for the defence of the action. Macmillan shall pay all resulting damages and costs awarded against Licensee but shall not be responsible for any settlement made without its consent. Macmillan may, at its option and expense: (i) replace or modify Software so that infringement will not exist; (ii) remove Software involved and refund Licensee a portion of the price paid therefore as depreciated or amortised by an equal annual amount over the lifetime of the Software as established by Macmillan; or (iii) obtain for Licensee the right to continue using the Software. Macmillan and its third party licensors disclaim all other liability for copyright, patent or other infringement, including any incidental or consequential damages. Macmillan shall have no liability for any infringements or claims thereof based upon: (i) the combination of Software with products not supplied by Macmillan, (ii) modification or alteration of Software by Macmillan in accordance with Licensee's instructions or by parties other than Macmillan, or (iii) failure to install updates provided by Macmillan.

7. TERM AND TERMINATION

7.1 This Licence shall become effective upon Software shipment and terminate at such time as Licensee discontinues use of Software on the Configuration, or upon sale, lease, or transfer by operation of law or otherwise, of the Configuration.
7.2 If Licensee fails to cure any breach of this Agreement, including failure to pay any required licence fees, within ten (10) days after receipt of written notice of such breach, the licence(s) as to which the breach exists shall be terminated.
7.3 Upon termination of any licence, Licensee shall immediately terminate use of Software for which the licence has been terminated and immediately either return or destroy all copies of such Software and other proprietary materials and certify in writing as to such destruction or return. Sections 3, 4, and 5 shall survive termination of this Agreement.

8. NON-WAIVER

The failure or delay of either party to exercise any right or remedy provided for herein shall not be deemed a waiver of that right or of any other rights or remedies available hereunder.

9. MISCELLANEOUS

9.1 Licensee agrees not to export Software, or re-export or resell Software from or in country of installation, without first complying with all applicable export laws and regulations. The Software may not be downloaded into any country which the United Kingdom has prohibited export.
9.2 Software support shall be provided under terms and conditions specified and in a separately executed Macmillan Software located in Support Agreement.
9.3 Where Licensee is located in the United States, its agencies or instrumentalities whether located within or outside of the United States, all Software and Documentation furnished hereunder is Commercial Computer Software and Commercial Computer Software Documentation provided only with the rights specified in this SLA customarily provided to the public by Macmillan in accordance with FAR 12.212 (a) and (b) (OCT 1995) or DFARS 227.7202-3(a) (JUN 1995) as applicable.
9.4 The Software may contain an electronic version of this SLA intended to have the same force and effect as a hardcopy SLA.
9.5 This Agreement shall be governed by English law. The United Nations Convention on Contracts for the International Sale of Goods is specifically disclaimed. Licensee's order documents shall state that the terms and conditions of this Agreement are the sole terms and conditions governing such order. This SLA states the entire understanding between the parties as to Software licensed by Licensee and shall take precedence over any omitted, conflicting or additional terms in any Licensee purchase order. If any provision of this SLA is determined to be invalid or unenforceable by a court of competent jurisdiction hereunder, the remaining provisions of this SLA shall not be affected and shall remain in full force and effect as though said invalid or unenforceable provision were not contained herein. The English language version of this Macmillan End-User Software Licence Agreement shall prevail and any translation into other languages other than English is for convenience only. No third party may enforce any of its terms under the Contracts (Rights of Third Parties) Act 1999.
9.6 Written notices required by this SLA shall be sent to the following:
Legal Department
Macmillan Publishers Ltd
4 Crinan Street
London N1 9XW
United Kingdom
9.7 Notwithstanding anything to the contrary provided herein, in the event of a change in control of all or substantially all of the assets of Macmillan, Macmillan may assign any or all of the rights and obligations under this Agreement to its successor in interest or to a third part assignee.

This product contains Adobe® AIR™ Runtime by Adobe® Systems Incorporated. All rights reserved. Adobe® and Adobe® AIR™ are trademarks of Adobe® Systems Incorporated.

© Macmillan Publishers Limited 2014

Macmillan Education
The Macmillan Building, 4 Crinan Street, London N1 9XW
A division of Macmillan Publishers Limited
Companies and representatives throughout the world

ISBN 978-0-230-43787-6

Written by Robert Grout, JoAnn Miller and Rhona Snelling
Text, design and illustration © Macmillan Publishers Limited 2014
Student's Book material © John Allison and Paul Emmerson

The authors have asserted their rights to be identified as the authors of this
work in accordance with the Copyright, Designs and Patents Act 1988.

First published 2014

Designed by emc design limited
Cover design by Keith Shaw, Threefold Design Limited
Cover image: Getty Images/RunPhoto
Audio recorded and produced by James Richardson Production Limited
Videos recorded and produced by Tom, Dick and Debbie Limited
Software developed by MPS Limited

The author and publishers would like to thank the following for permission
to reproduce their photographs:

Icons throughout: Brand X Pictures(watch), Getty(tests, grammar help,
contents map), ImageSource(writing tips), Macmillan Publishers Ltd(dictionary),
Photoalto(language practice, print & work), Photodisc(wordlist), Stockbyte(listen).

These materials may contain links for third party websites. We have no control over,
and are not responsible for, the contents of such third party websites. Please use
care when accessing them.

Although we have tried to trace and contact copyright holders before publication,
in some cases this has not been possible. If contacted we will be pleased to rectify
any errors or omissions at the earliest opportunity.

Printed and bound in Thailand

2018 2017 2016 2015 2014
10 9 8 7 6 5 4 3 2 1